Scribe Publications
THE TASTE OF RIVER WATER

Cate Kennedy is the author of the highly acclaimed novel *The World Beneath*, which won the People's Choice Award in the NSW Premier's Literary Awards in 2010 and was shortlisted for many other prizes, including *The Age* Book of the Year. She is also an award-winning short-story writer whose work has been published widely. Her collection, *Dark Roots*, was shortlisted for the Steele Rudd Award in the Queensland Premier's Literary Awards and for the Australian Literature Society Gold Medal. Cate is also the author of the travel memoir *Sing, and Don't Cry*, and the poetry collections *Joyflight*, *Signs of Other Fires* and *The Taste of River Water*, which won the Victorian Premier's Literary Award for Poetry in 2011. She lives on a secluded bend of the Broken River in north-east Victoria.

The Taste of River Water
CATE KENNEDY

Scribe Publications Pty Ltd
18–20 Edward St, Brunswick, Victoria 3056, Australia
50A Kingsway Place, Sans Walk, London, EC1R 0LU, United Kingdom

First published by Scribe 2011
Reprinted 2011, 2012, 2013
This edition published 2014

Typeset in 10.75/14 pt Minion by the publishers.
Printed and bound in England by CPI Group (UK) Ltd.

Some of these poems have been previously published:
'How to eat a guava' in *Signs of Other Fires* (Five Islands Press);
and 'Joy flight', 'Picasso's portrait of a young woman', 'Mud wasps',
'The Poor Commissioners', 'Thinking the room empty', 'Love and work',
'Making a path' and 'Namaste' in *Joyflight* (Interactive Press).

National Library of Australia
Cataloguing-in-Publication data

Kennedy, Cate.

The Taste of River Water.

9781922247407 (pbk.)

A821.4

This project has been assisted by
the Australian government through
the Australia Council for the Arts,
its arts funding and advisory body.

Australian Government

Australia Council for the Arts

scribepublications.com.au
scribepublications.co.uk

Here, there is no edge for cutting, and no garde
for avanting, there is only the same old story,
fresh as resurrection

— Kristin Henry, 'This story'

Contents

III

Letter (1)

At college, we practised sound editing on reel-to-reels,
doctoring famous speeches with a razor blade and tape,
slicing out silences and stumbles
from our own garrulous recordings of each other.

Stuck to the table edge would be a dangling fringe of pieces,
ready to be spliced together:
sometimes a long eloquent sentence,
sometimes just a useful, crisp connective,
an *and* or *so you see ...*
and a box of the out-takes:
tongue-tied throat clearings,
clicks, coughs, suppressed laughter,
the thick dead air between pronouncements
as we lost our thread, rattled by the microphone.

I find I've carried it with me,
this box of shining, static fragments,
along with a roll of editing tape
and the endless sifting and fossicking required
to join each small piece together into a single sequence
ribboning through the spool like a narrow dark river.

Turns out I've saved each mortifying, blurting hesitation,
starting and restarting,
the ragged edge, imperfectly cut and joined
making a sound like someone swallowing.

So I snatch moments to do this:
incising one piece
and bending to the screen again,

frowning, coffee in hand,
to select another —
they're lined up faithfully here somewhere —
I've lost my system,
endlessly distracted
by the tape and razor blades of the larger world.

But nothing is discarded,
give me long enough
and I'll have this gift for you assembled ready:

a spliced symphony of lapses, of the truest silences
broken only by the sound of someone
with a lump in their throat.

I

Thinking the room empty

I am being told a long story of a chain of coincidences.
A friend, losing her way in the desert,
walks out of a dry Alice Springs riverbed into
thirty thousand miles
of flat ruled horizon, blazing heat, waterless saltbush.

She finds a fence and walks along it.
A sign tells her she has reached a rifle range
and, in the distance, the mirage shimmer of a tin shed.
She is thirsty, and she trespasses
climbs through the fence
walks expecting rifle fire
forces the door.

In the dimness she finds nothing but a big empty crate,
and abandoned, waiting silence.
She has one chance, and she sees it.
She takes the crate outside, stands it on end, climbs it,
and pulls herself onto the roof of the shed.
Turning in a slow 360 degrees she catches sight
of the low mountain range she recognises as north
elevated over the line of the horizon —
the direction back to town —
sets off, swallowing dust,
weak with relief.

The point of the story is yet to come — the birth of her daughter
brought about by a lift, once she found the road back to town,
from a stranger she flagged down, and so forth —
I listen, but part of my mind
stays lingering in the gloom with that crate

and her presence of mind, stilling panic,
recognising it for what it was.

I wonder how many times I have broken some lock,
searched hastily and withdrawn,
thinking the room empty,
overlooked the disguised and waiting gift,
missed the mountain.

I wonder what my stunted sightline
has failed to notice
what path home
I have abandoned.

Joy flight

My father's stories must be provoked from him
by some landslide of sorrow;
a lost city's foundations revealed by shifting earth.
Only after the death of two brothers
does he relate some childhood moment
of a Sunday after Mass, when a Tiger Moth
touched down on a patch of ground
offering joy flights.

I see them, those three blond boys taut with longing,
that silver machine, the sky.
My father remembers the sum of money required
for the three boys to go up
and his own father's face, closed and abashed,
after he asked the pilot.
He turned away,
and my father steeled himself for the walk home to lunch.
Yet somehow his father was carrying the money,
and somehow he decided.
They flew.

Disaster could have struck,
and sent my grandmother mad with grief.
My grandfather would have been condemned
to watch that, from the ground, forever.
But nothing went wrong.
They flew, and returned safely to the earth, transformed,
an awestruck moment in a poor childhood,
desire made real, a stern father hiding his smile on the run home.

Everyone who witnessed that event is dead now.
My father handed me the story, a small recovered legacy,
glinting and bright with disuse.
Now I carry those three buffeted, grinning children
in their Sunday clothes,
hardly able to believe their luck,
astonished by joy and flight.

I hold this, and yearn to write fiction
in the face of these deaths and losses,
in the face of all that is forgotten
and revealed by the stark shift of pain and surprise.
I want to carry this talisman carved like a rune
for my father, for my uncles, for my grandfather,
and for that pilot;
for that pure torn-open moment
where they each slipped free of the earth.
Fiction, which is the ribbon pulled from a trembling mouth,
which tells its truth with such defiance
that everything forgotten will blaze, every joy burnished,
every recollection of unexpected flight shared
and passed from hand to cupped hand,
carried warm next to the skin,
recited for courage.

Picasso's portrait of a young woman

A trip to the city.
A family wanders past the floral clock
when a light rain
drives them inside the art gallery.

Her sister wants to look at the atrium's stained-glass ceiling
and run her fingers along the mesmerising water
streaming down the plate-glass doors.
Her mother browses in the foyer shop for gift cards.
Desultory, they follow the crowds through the exhibit doors,
filling in time until the weather clears.

In the first gallery they come across a retrospective of drawings
by Picasso, recently dead and deified,
the dizzying output of a loose, utterly confident pencil.
Her mother whispers to her father
that they hardly seem worth framing.
The child stares through the shifting bodies of milling adults
at Picasso's portrait of a young woman.

As her family makes a cursory circuit of the bulls and battles,
she looks at the eyes, the two u-shapes making irises
the five eyelashes stalks of crayon, pure and precise
the mouth swept in a bow in four strokes
the whole face a single flourish of careless joy.

Something closes in her throat, then opens.
A hand somewhere
sweeps a piercing, unerring line through her chest.

The rain has stopped.
Her sister and parents return,
promising a visit to the donut van before they go to the car.
As they walk out she cannot name the change, the dislocation.
It is as if the lozenges of light in that foyer ceiling
have been reassembled, the blood beats in her head
as though newly transfused, these people strangers,
speaking a dulled and muffled language.

Those eyes under their winged brows, grave and perfect,
watch everything with their luminous compassion.
They have seen before what they see now;
a child, suddenly subdued,
something inside swept raw and newly secretive
judging now, silently,
what must be kept hidden to survive;
the vigilant camouflage of thorn bushes
the grim survey lines of loneliness it will require.

Almost drowning

An undertow relies on our amnesia.
Despite seeing the beach carved thin
by this same current,
we still wade in.

We are not mindful
of this restless body of water,
clearing us out of the way
with the side of its hard hand.
We stroll into it absently, eyes caught
by some brief crushed-glass sheen,
dulled like acolytes are dulled
by the easy recitation of prayer.

So, you are swimming, speechless and immersed,
beginning to realise
you are floundering on some deep fault line.

Carried backwards like this,
you must swim diagonally to the rip,
not back to shore, which seems insane;

but with this single shred of remembered knowledge
you are swimming with everything you have,
losing your footing and losing face
and, at last, losing oxygen.

When you, finally, raise that flagging arm to call for help,
accept that never again will you be so eloquent
this is your moment, after all,
for every eloquence you can muster,

every hour you have ever spent learning language
has been for this, and nothing more:
to pronounce the simple words you need
perfectly and comprehensibly, across the swell.

You cannot risk being misheard or misconstrued
each word you can bear to utter —
urgent, desperate, humble —
is your lifebuoy
your thrown rope
a jacket inflating like lungs.

Before the rip pulls you under,
draw breath, and confess
that you are nothing in the face of this
that you are spent.
Vow, fervently, to stand witness to this
if you are only allowed back on solid ground.

Do this every morning
every page
every penstroke.
There is no other way, trust me.
Trust my sustaining arm
my words, breathed back
into your mouth
the salt drying on our faces.

How to eat a guava

First rinse the fruit, rub the skin and inhale
make an incision with the eye tooth
a bite with a seesawing motion to break
that curved yellow moon surface
eat it
like you would kiss a long-lost lover
like you would taste the skin behind an ear
you cannot worry
about juice
separate the seeds from the flesh with your tongue
sift them down your throat
recall custard in expensive affair-soaked hotels
lemon mousse drowning the mouth
in reckless garden sunsweat tussles
eat it
like you would plunge into a river in moonlight
like you would open your mouth and let the river in
like you would eat a stolen pear, a hot fig lush as a lovebite
eat it
like you would crush it onto skin, lower your head
confusing perfume with texture, tasting scent
under a collarbone, like you would lick a line of sweat up a spine
bite skin, flesh, seeds, juice
eat it fast
like you were ravenous
parched, gluttonous, flushed with secrecy
eat it slowly
lick your fingers

Mud wasps

Before we fitted the window,
the mud wasps came
as they had for years,
and made a bulbous nest on the brick wall.

All through the hammering of ceiling rafters and roof
I watched them,
striped and gleaming like poisonous sweets, legs dangling,
droning in and out of the wall cavity
with their wet balls of mud,
patting it layer by scrupulous layer into a nest.

Those busy, impossible abdomens,
connected with a fine-threaded needle to thorax,
curved over as they worked.
The framing finished, the newly glazed window
sealed and polished, showed us sky and river
contained like a postcard.

It is our territory now, lined with bookshelves and carpet,
and the nest has stayed there, sequestered, all through winter,
swelling unnoticed high up against the bricks.
Seven months have passed, and now wasps
are hitting against the glass outside, feeling around
this barrier to their remembered flight path.
Two wasps have blundered through the house
incongruous as helicopters,
clawing hunched at closed windows everywhere.

In the mud nest,
two perfectly round holes.

I hesitate, here with my kitchen knife and dustpan,
frightened of what lies walled up in there;
something cramped and fully grown
waiting to be released
winged and barbed and shining like armour

and still, outside the window,
that insistent knocking,
come to claim what is theirs.

Binaries

In my parents' lounge room, after Christmas lunch,
I am listening to my brother, the computer programmer,
explaining the principles of cyberspace.

'It's basically a system of binaries,' he says,
'permutations of zero and one. So the data
may be stored as, say, zero zero one one one, zero zero one.'

My mother sighs, next to us on the couch.
She is knitting a cable-knit cardigan.
'You kids,' she says.
'I'll never understand how you get your brains around it.
It's beyond me.'

And she turns back to her knitting,
purl purl plain plain plain, purl purl plain.

Making a path

We are crouched in do-it-yourself land,
arguing over preparation and degrees of finish,
rolling brickies' sand smooth as a piecrust.

These bricks are salvaged,
they have all been handled and rehandled —
we are saving ourselves thirty dollars an hour
to learn the hard way about warp and imperfection.
The pattern is a herringbone.
It seems so simple.

We graze our hands, raise calluses, crawl like penitents.
This pattern veers away from right angles,
you can't cut them to fit, they are fired that way —
adjust your string-lines
adjust them, or shut up.

We have stopped talking.
Your mouth makes its odd line
as you smack the bricks I've laid
with the rubber mallet.
We only have one of these
we must take it in turns
to impose our versions of what's correct.

We cross each other's shadows,
yearning for the soft sand and the broom —
that sweet curve disappearing around the corner,
soft groundcovers hiding our errors.
You stretch your spine, melancholy with your own thoughts,
I suck a blood blister raised by the nip of cruel stone.

We knock off mortar with chisels,
the rasping echoes like throat-clearing.

We will invite others to walk on this
as if making it was effortless.
I crawl forward brick by misshapen brick
already knowing this
already forgiving us
our small and fallible trespasses.

Locusts arrive in the city

Locusts arrive in the city,
having eaten the countryside bare on the way,
thrumming through the thick air like cargo carriers,
carapaces crackling, and mandibles like a miracle of nature
jawing back and forth like a typewriter carriage
knocking out pulp fiction in a sweaty fifties hotel room
the overhead fan clacking like a million transparent wings.
Locusts arrive in the city,
a rippling forward offensive ordered by a crazed general
waving one barbed leg,
hard and helmeted and identical,
with heavy windscreen casualties,
their enemy's metal shells glitter in the broil
mirage heat rises from the battlefield.
They have devoured everything in their path
and like any army, they turn to the prize of the city now
with mindless, covetous eyes,
a trail of famine in their wake,
carolling havoc, insane with hunger,
down to the wire.
They will not seem like the agents of death,
smashing into harmless protein against your radiator grille
or ricocheting into your supersized coffee
as you dream away your hot lunch-hour on a bench,
but look up, at sunset, and here comes the wilderness
pouring through some rent in the balance sheet.
Go ahead — put your hand over your cup.
The potboiler is almost finished,
and it ends badly.

How to play Marineboy

What did I know, what did I know
of love's austere and lonely offices?
Robert Hayden, 'Those Winter Sundays'

First what you need
is a Clarke's two-foot-six backyard swimming pool,
gleaming surreal aqua in the dead rectangle
of brown summer grass
between the Hill's Hoist and the shed —
this will be Marineboy's universe.
Next you need a bucket of water
to dunk your feet into before you climb in:
this water must be blood-warm,
full of floating specks of mown grass;
your dad has an idea it keeps grass and dirt out of the pool,
which he has also chlorinated so heavily
his kids' hair is gradually turning green.

Early mornings, in the cool, he is out there,
netting leaves off the surface
in a gesture children do not recognise yet as love.

So get into the water and wade around,
swan forward into the soupy blue.
You must hold your nose
when you attempt the backward somersault
and thresh around the edges to form a sluggish whirlpool —
when you cast yourself into it
close your eyes
scream.

Now you are ready to become Marineboy.
Unwrap a Wrigley's Spearmint chewing-gum stick,
say: 'Now I must take an oxytab.'
Chew it, dive to rescue and escape,
aching with the belief that you can breathe underwater.
You are in the Coral Kingdom now,
twisting and falling like reckless dolphins,
forests of seaweed wave overhead as you breathe
sweet spearmint
and harness seahorses.

Wet each foot carefully,
before you enter this benign and weightless element,
this small blue oasis.
Oh, we do not recognise it yet
we do not recognise it.

8 x 10 colour enlargements $16.50

Let me lay it out for you:
a rural photography competition in a local town hall
and the woman next to me,
sitting with her husband and two children,
had travelled three hours to be there.

Her kids were quiet
with the soft, cowed politeness of remote life,
a farm up in the lonely dry stretch of the western districts,
her husband's boots smelling of polish,
and he, preoccupied as the judge made her speech,
thinking no doubt of the work waiting for him back at home
and the cost of filling up the car to return.

He looked at his hands on his knees
and then over at the photos on the wall —
the 'dead-tree-silhouette-and-sunset' photos
the 'cobweb-misted-with-dew-at-dawn' photos —
as his wife drank it all in hungrily
and then stood to be awarded second prize.

I want you to imagine
the brief economical smile they exchanged
when she sat down again, holding her certificate —
her landscape photo on display carefully mounted on card,
enlarged at the chemist's in town,
budgeted for, cautiously admired.
The judge announced the winning photo,
a massive sunset shot, the colours juiced with Photoshop,
someone else stood for that applause and that cheque.

Then the judge added, in passing,
that there'd been another photo she'd admired,
which would have been a winner
except its theme was not 'Images of Rural Life'
as specified in the competition rules,
and she held up a picture of the woman's two children
gazing transfixed out of a window,
the light pouring in, their faces upturned with wonder,
and the woman stood again
and politely collected this photograph,
tucked it with the certificate on her lap,
saying nothing.

Later, as her husband checked his watch,
and spoke softly to his kids, a hand on his daughter's fair head,
I told her how much I loved the picture
and what a wonderful photographer I thought she was,
and she smiled and looked at her photo.
'You know,' she said, 'it didn't break the rules.
This was the first moment my children ever saw rain.'

They left then,
back to their car, to the long drive home,
to the big bone-dry expanse of land beyond salvaging
with a second-prize certificate
and so few words between them

no speaking up
no protest or complaint
no claim of being wronged, or misrepresented

but I think, even now,
about how the light streamed onto her children's rapt faces,
the tired love in her husband's hand,
and her, running to find her camera and frame it
the smell of the rain-marked dust
rare momentary joy.

They left, and all this passed into silence:
unremarked and unacknowledged,
that's why I'm telling you now.

After the deconsecration

At the appointed hour, a crowd gathers in the cold,
waiting, sombre in the face of ritual, huddled in black coats,
here in this yard where Mass and funerals,
christenings and Christmas
have pulled congregations together for a century.

No bell, this morning.
The bell's already gone.
At nine a.m. the auctioneer arrives,
and his silent workers, like boys solemn with the responsibility
of the book, the chalice, the crucifix,
unlock the church, and carry out the first of the pews.

The yard hasn't seen a crowd like this for years.
The priest would smile a rueful, bitter smile
if there was still a priest.

First, there's fierce bidding for the marble font.
The man who buys it rests an owner's hand on it, unsmiling
as the men come forward to lift it away.
Each pew, brought forward one at a time,
goes to antique dealers or collectors with long verandahs,
who will point out the carving to customers,
pat the pews like curios,
like rocking horses, like hope chests.

Apart from these transactions, no one speaks.
This is our call and response now, our mannered piety
as our voices rise in testimony and grave-faced reverence.

Away from the business at hand, inside the old church
the statuary has gone, in case of thieving,
the Stations of the Cross are stacked in the narthex,
and swallows roost in the vandal-repellent wire mesh
protecting the single stained-glass window
intact for a hundred years,
bought with parish pledges, and shipped from Germany.
A heritage group has duly checked it over, and declared it
unremarkable.

I am trespassing across this burnished slab of basalt
where believers paused to dip tentative fingers into that font,
being hauled, now, onto someone's trailer with rope,
the prayers recited out there
so full of vigorous certitude.
In here, in the cold derelict light,
the trace of old incense reminds me
of how early people carried fire;
twisting grass into a green nest
then wrapping one slow-burning coal
for the long walk ahead.

I think my hands would know how to do this
like the ghost of an old, fervent memory —
I think, if that auctioneer would just shut up,
that both of us could stoop
to nurture a small salvaged coal with our breath,
seeing it glow and smoulder just enough
that our eyes would lock above it
mute with the miracle of comprehension.

Last man standing

His eyes had a farsighted serenity even as a child,
anxious to smile in the studio photo in his best clothes:
a hand-knitted school jumper, too-big shirt collar,
small hands resting empty and scrubbed,
a mouth learning to keep its hopes to itself.

He showed me another picture,
emulsion cracking over the creases, worn thin:
ten men in shorts and boots grinning in blinding desert sun
standing on a wrecked tank holding crowbars.
He said: *They sent us in right after detonation —*
that metal was still too damn hot to touch.

Hot, molten with half-life,
the whole area was ticking hot in 1956,
billowing with megaton clouds and irradiated red dust.
His fingers smoothed the edges gently,
thumb passing over those lost open faces.
I'm the only one left alive of all that mob.

Somewhere in behind his eyes,
it was there, moving leisurely from tongue to throat to bone
something dark on the x-rays
splaying up towards his brain
like seepage from a poisoned well.

Radiation therapy was never going to halt it.
He must have considered this irony,
lying there as other experts
pressed buttons and watched from a distance —
this time in lead-lined aprons instead of uniforms,

hesitating
before they touched him.

After they'd taken out part of his jaw and cheekbone
he shuffled, face caved and disfigured, into the backyard,
thinking to move the sprinklers,
and the kids next door cried when they saw him;
cowed as the Elephant Man, he stumbled back inside
and asked his wife to make him a hood.

When he grinned,
it pulled the side of his broken face up into a rictus;
nothing else of that suntanned boy was visible by then
except the sky-bleached eyes
that quietly assessed the arid landscape
and saw that he was done with the tests and the Commission,
the Appeals Tribunal, compensation, the Ministry;
saw that none of them would live to see it told.

He stared into that blinding horror without flinching
and pulled his big flat cap more firmly down
on his scarred misshapen head
to spare us the sight.

Towards the end, palate and tongue destroyed,
mute on the hospice bed as an old green fan
stirred the air around,
he gave up trying to sound the words.
Instead he held an exercise book,
each page with its humble telegram of residual, spiky dignity
like a needle on a counter,

measuring and clicking still after all these years:
I would like a drink
painkiller
no thank you
no more
he found a blank page, and wrote to me, the pencil jerking:
don't want to go blind

The thought of being mute and blind
with the tumour crawling up behind your eyes:
this made me take his hand
as both of us prayed fiercely, silently, for his death.
He fumbled for a fresh page
to write a note about life insurance and his wife's pension,
and passed over
not too bad today
sleeping pill, please
thank you
and the blotched page that said: *I have had enough*

The desert, in the end, had to use its older weapons —
exhaustion, thirst and hunger, surrender —
to claim him.
He walked out there into that toxic mirage,
getting on with the job, no rage or questions,
squinting into the strewn wreckage
flash-burned red across the brow
already marked with invisible ash.

He would have gone calmly.
You can see it in the blond boy in that first photo,

gravely gazing into the distance
as if he can already make out, on the horizon,
the dazzling shape
of what was to be delivered to him.

The Poor Commissioners

In 1849 a group of 150 famine victims were denied sustenance at the poorhouse in Westport, County Mayo, Ireland, until they had registered with the so-called 'Poor Commissioners', based fourteen miles away at Delphi House. In the depths of winter they walked there through the valley by Croagh Patrick, Ireland's Holy Mountain, only to find that the commissioners were having dinner and would not see them. Dozens froze to death in the snow. A stone monument on the place today reads: 'To commemorate the Hungry Poor who walked here in 1849, and walk the Third World today.'

And what were they thinking, finally, as they sank down,
hope extinguished,
or was it a relief to stop thinking
only reeling, drifting in and out in the whirling sleet,
glimpsing your father there, huddled, vanishing
so that the snow at last, a misjudged enemy,
invited you down to rest,
muffling each voice
and a faint half-dreamed comfort in closing your eyes
on your knees in the shadow of the Croagh,
named for the saint who fasted, like Our Saviour,
only both from choice.

Beyond bitter curses, then, or did they die raging,
snot and tears freezing on their faces?
Who was chosen to muster a semblance of dignity
to approach the house,
and how to return
to break the news to the others,
and with what words?

And the men in the house, never dreaming
that this would be the moment seized by fate to expose them,
this, which was commonplace, no doubt;
they were Commissioners, only that,
righteous with due process,
stamps and nibs put away for the day, and now
dealing with a nuisance, irritable,
pushing the last of the bread around their plate.

Would they have behaved better
if they knew they were to be judged?
Jumped to stoke the fire,
order a tureen of soup made,
swing open those doors,
be exemplary?
History catches us like this,
buttons undone and disguises off
aggrieved with burdensome paperwork,
maintaining order in some godforsaken outpost
and, frankly, the poor always with us.

And so these hundred and fifty, unnamed,
condemned to white oblivion by a flat refusal,
one stone, now, suffices for them all.

It is the past we find containable
folded along old certainties
like a map or a card;
a stone to mark distance,
reduced to well-worn lines,
observed through a square glass pane:

the Hungry Poor, outside the gates at Delphi House,
the villains and the victims,
the snow soaked with amnesia,
frozen here and rendered into monochrome
by this driving rain.

But they are with us,
trudging with the last of their energy,
thousands of miles now, from poorhouses and famine fields,
chilled and exiled, holding pitchforks or children
or unsigned paperwork,
forged, faded identifications, the wrong currencies,
they are with us and we will not see them
as they come through the valley,
spurred by a mirage of lit windows
and laughable hopes of some borrowed hearth,
they are with us, and we are done with them,
we will not meet their eyes.

Tomorrow we will draw a red line in the ledger,
pious and put-upon, holding this burden like a full plate
against our memory of the cold.

This is Delphi of the silenced, unrecognisable stones,
where witness is a frozen and thawed and refrozen thing,
Delphi, where the oracle speaks, and we do not listen.

Suspect

How adept we must become
at reading calluses
and the thin curling straps of mended sandals.

His wife or sister
carefully washed those cotton clothes clean
sometime last week, humming,
and the darned sweater his trembling son wears
speaks volumes to us, in knobbled wool and holes.

I have learned to search now
for different details to make my judgements:
reading innocence in broken fingernails
the delicate exposed skin
on the cowed, tender neck
of a six-year-old boy,
innocence in his father's clasping hands, gentling him.
This helps me imagine
bedtime stories, soft voices, normalcy.

For this man, at least, I fought
to compose a story,
something ending,
after this nauseating wait, pushed into the Iraqi dust,
in an admission of patent error
then apology and release.

I had no choice: they had tied a black bag
over his defeated head, so
I could not tell from his face.

Namaste

My right hand floats out to greet everything —
the curving hand carved on the stone knee
of the Egyptian temple god on exhibit
at the Metropolitan Museum in New York,
the perfect lintel over the door of an oratory,
its stones fitted together like teeth,
the letters of the first Celtic alphabet on a tablet
barely there now, eroded into air and words.

Three thousand years, twelve hundred, eight hundred —
it all melts away,
their hand holding the chisel and my hand empty,
our fingers closing together on this,
this offering, this love letter, this moment, this marvel.
I greet all these labours of love,
all these hands moving, synchronous, in sign language
through mediums more durable than one lifetime.

Our fingertips touch
through chilled stone,
the church a ruin, the museum
guarded with lasers.
We call our greetings and farewells,
we call thank you, outstretched and faint,
yearning across darkness like an empty field,
lowering our arms finally,
and turning back, treading blindly
towards the window-lit house
the unimaginable future.

Quiet

turn it off

listen to the cicadas
listen to that knock of branches
listen just to the wind —
here it is, rolling now
like a pitching wave into the trees
erasing the crazed and cross-tracked footprints of static

in what you took for silence
listen to the dry wood
catching, at this perfect moment, in the stove

stop, and you'll hear it;
the stretch and crack and tick
of the thin metal flue
expanding in the heat

oh, you are beaten so thin
and still the joins hold,
still that bloom of warmth
opening up
more than enough

and your hands
still feeling the shape
of the kindling, the axe, the tree;
the flexing
of your own bird-fine bones.

II

Eating earth

There are new words to learn.
Surfactant:
the doctor says it, the midwives
whose hands slip through the blanket to stroke my foot
as I see my baby thrashing in distress on the ultrasound —
the lungs are too premature to have developed surfactant.
Had my waters broken four weeks hence
all might have been different.
Instead they break now
my boy is born drowned
still and perfect.

All night
a saline drip ticks like a clock into my hand
tear by tear.

Later at home, I observe my beaten body,
heavy as a hole in space,
helplessly pulling towards itself, in the airless dark,
every black and icy satellite imaginable.

Pica:
a disorder where expectant mothers eat clay,
craving the taste of soil and earth.
Every morning waking is like going through a windscreen,
retching on a mouthful of invisible grit,
cold metal probing on the same throbbing nerve.

my child died

I am pushing on some simmering splinter,
some fragment of burning shrapnel,
reopening flesh over and over.
I want this cauterised, branded into me,
a hard and desensitised scar,
stopping all assumption in its shocked tracks.

my child died

I am eating dirt, drinking it.
Dusty water swills my clenching mouth,
tongue-tied by this new language,
beside this sundered shore
of silt, salt, mica,

and inside this traitorous skin
appearing so benignly whole
concealing such treacherous, eroded gullies.

Taproot

I must plant the tree seedling
a friend left here on the step
find a place for the cards.

It seems important somehow
a matter of fumbling pride
to fold all this paper square for recycling
the florist wrap from such extravagant, unwanted flowers
the envelopes
I'm saving the envelopes
I forget why for the minute.

The book says: do one small thing a day
there is nothing to do but be patient
as if I were recovering, stunned, from a stroke.

I pick up a cup carefully
watch the hand with the fork blindly jab something on the plate
wait immobilised, lobotomised, humble
until I remember how to move one foot forward.

Soon I will rise and find a spade
pull on my boots and plant that tree seedling
find a pen and paper
note down the return addresses on those envelopes
write and thank people for their sympathy.

Pretty soon now
cradling my whole body like a dislocated bone.

In that pot, the longer I wait
a taproot searching for water
is beginning to curl back upon itself.

I sit unmoved, visualising it:
white and ragged
blind with pot-bound constriction.

Soon I will rise
pen and paper
envelopes
spade
the unbearable sight
of turned earth.

Windburn

If you are worn brittle with each other,
do not be lured by the thought of a swim in waves,
in clean, purifying salt.
Glazed with sweat and pounded with headache light,
we even found the route there a sore point:
the missed freeway exits
like needles of glass under the skin,
a road metaphor so hackneyed our lips were stiff with shame.

A front beach contains no shelter, and no mercy.
We swam buffeted between narrow, snapping flags,
thrashing to stay on our feet
as a vast rip sucked the headland —
your solitary dark head ducking beyond the breakers,
those flags red rags to you —
then dragged ourselves back into baked and glazed traffic,
and a jackhammer orange sun obliterating all westerly vision.

What do you nurse tonight?
For myself, I have this sandblasted flesh
and the tiny sea-smoothed comfort
of a single moment between us
as we stood under the beach shower in the wind,
its water blowing horizontally like a vapour trail,
a fleeting exchanged smile
that I hoard in my pocket
like the last shell in the world,
and this rim of salt on my forearm
like unnoticed, evaporated tears,
as if I've spent today silent, unconsolable,
weeping into the crook of my elbow.

Bushfires, it turned out, had ringed the whole coast that day.
That explained, at least, the churning sea,
the bitter taste of smoke from the smudged horizon,
the scorched seed cones of remnant banksia
prised open now, like jaws.

Love and work

The moment will come, next year or else today,
no one talks about it, but it's true:
grief is work — implacable, in our way,
a snarled, exhausting thing we need to do.
It waits for us. We'd rather it grew weeds
like a burned-down house, or rusted wreck,
than see its scalded bulk beneath the reeds
and haul its wreckage up onto the deck.
And grief is like Pompeii, each shard a clue
to be painfully recovered on our knees,
no one talks about it, but it's true:
we must kneel down and name it piece by piece.
We falter at the task that lies at hand,
the hard-won pattern we must pick apart
the broken glass that we must sift like sand
the knives we turn on our constricted heart
and all the bloodless scars we hoped to leave —
we do not get to shirk, or even choose
to see the world the way we would believe.
This world which uses us. This world we use.
Love and work, Freud tells us, is the cure
but love, this tapped vein that has bled too much,
has left us just with work, and now I fear
the toxic half-life of this thing still warm to touch.
Darkness hides the waiting shapes of day
that will lie there till we steel ourselves to start.
Here comes the light. We cannot turn away —
seeing is the hardest but most necessary part.

Knothole

Last night, as I hauled a log onto the fire,
ants came pouring from a knothole, racing from the flame.
I took a stick and propped it like a drawbridge for them
against the hearth.

Then my hand reached out
and knocked it away again.

I can't explain the heavy somnolence, predatory and feline,
which overtook me.
My luxuriating in it.
The stick in my hand as ants swarmed wildly,
beyond rescue.

I just stood with what I had done
as the house around me filled with things not said,
each room infested with the shapes of something small but alive
and desperately fleeing.

The shortest day of the year

The bare ash tree stands whipped by a dry winter,
its branches exposing every abandoned nest
the summer leaves once hid.

This should be easy.
Nature's like therapy,
everybody writes about trees:
those branches wait for me
to compare them to a defiant fist,
a hand stretched in entreaty,
anything
but words are failing me,
every time I stand here
my eye is snagged by the nests there in the branches,
revealed now as what they are:
derelict and untidy clumps of grass.

Knock one down and all that remains within
is a small misshapen hollow,
those remnant feathers laid inside
having outlived their usefulness.

I should be sweeping
but instead I'm standing, king-hit, holding the broom,
staring at that tree,
every gust of wind reminding me
like a cold hectoring poke to the chest
that the world owes me nothing.

Snow

This cold, this leaden lethargy
can only be hypothermia.
Think about it:
confusion, *exhaustion*, *impaired judgement*, *shivering*;
the urge to simply lie down, in some freezing, blinding drift,
and succumb to drowsy sleep at last.

Then there's the ache, or worse, the lack of ache,
the same dulled, deadened nerves of white amnesia
that asks only to leave the path
and sink down, exhausted, and rest.

Well, no more floundering for a diagnosis,
this is it: the turning away
from the crackling static of the disconnected screens,
the abandoned posts, everything cooling in the silence,
the sense of not being able to swallow any more.

Some official is snapping their fingers at us,
and we turn away, incoherent, nauseated, stumbling.
Don't you understand? We're so tired of being questioned,
our arms grabbed and tested for rigidity,
the quiet, concerned voices in the other room.
They shake their thermometers, frowning
at our irritable, distracted responses,
tick the box on their clipboard that says *unwilling to go on.*

No, it is snow we long for,
which asks nothing of us,
trampled and compressed with disoriented footprints
of all the deliriums that have come before us,

or maybe those staggering prints are our own —
we're too stupefied now to remember.
If we could just sleep,
serenely, perfectly still and quiet.

It drifts sweetly through us, this cloudy, indifferent anaesthetic,
as we step regretfully amid our scattered papers,
the bulletins and prescriptions and directives,
which rained down from the sky, urging us to surrender:
well, we are finally
compliantly
acquiescent.

You have your prognosis.
Leave us here then,
like Napoleon's poor exhausted soldiers,
our identifications soaked in our pockets,
our cheap uniforms a thin joke against the cold.
Leave us to succumb as our slurred speech
thickens gratefully into silence.

It's such a relief, to forget
the faintly recalled, pressing imperatives of our mission.
We turn our backs on the frantic morse of new dispatches,
the false news of victory,
the liberation on the ruined streets.
We deliver ourselves, instead, into this beautiful snow;
this painless rolling white, blotting all in its path
so clean and pure
so pitiless.

Breath

Firefighting gear is bundled by the door
in fluorescent five-alarm yellow,
every morning there's a pager test,
and the warning siren
sounds a sombre all-clear.

Each man in the crew, on tenterhooks,
waits for the continuous blaring wail,
in the tinder dry that aches to burn,
the scream that would herald disaster.

I practise starting the truck carrying the water tank,
stack towels ready to soak.
With each breath I can smell it:
smoke and dust,
knee-deep leaf litter crisped to shell.

On the fridge is the fire plan,
sensibly discussed and prioritised,
but were that fire to start
I doubt my rationality.
Like an idiot, I fear I would run,
an ant under the boiling sky,
for a shovel and a box
to dig up the small tree I keep alive with bathwater.

You hear, afterwards, this kind of ludicrous story,
a litany of preventable fatalities:
people's desperate, nonsensical actions,
turning back, like Lot's wife, to a burning house,
dying getting the dogs off their chains,

dying digging up some tree,
wasting minutes
as the elements roared closer, eating up the air itself,
the keys in the truck
waiting, untouched.

But in the face of such radiant heat
we may have a change of heart
about what is suddenly essential;
perhaps in those seconds
of fighting for breath
we see at last what we would die without
in the aftermath still to be borne.

It's not the conflagration,
just ask the experts:
it's the smoke that kills you,
not the flame.

Colostrum

Barely speaking,
we get the cow into the yard.
Her rejected calf lies stunned on the ground
like a wrinkled black coat dropped from a chair.

The cow's having none of it.
She swings at you, staggering but game,
roping you with slobber,
your shirt already slippery
with blood and shit.

The smell of afterbirth,
mammalian, unmistakeable,
makes us unable to look at each other.

Back lashes a furious hoof to sink into my shin.
It's almost a relief to allow pain
a hot, skin-broken focus
away from the sight of her desperate eye rolling,
the white of it curdled with intimate, exposed terror.
Push her up into the crush, you say.
Tie her leg out of the way.

We lift the flopping calf to her udder,
he sinks, wanting to sleep till death,
and buckles exhausted back into the dust.
And still, we cannot meet each other's eye.

We rouse him again.
His little mouth tries and tries to connect,
too small to even reach.

Now we both see what's ahead:
hand milking, and hand feeding,
the chore of keeping this one alive —
or just walk away
open the yard
let the cow stagger trembling to the shade of the tree
let the calf slip away.

His mouth opens.
Inside, his soft palate is rippled like a seabed,
he tries to nurse your fingers.
Get a teat, you say finally,
there's one in the kitchen drawer.

When I get back you've milked her,
and we tilt the calf's neck,
work a finger into the side of his mouth,
slide the teat inside for that first quick convulsive swallow;
your hands cradle the head
without a shred of sentimentality

I crouch there tipping that bottle of precious colostrum,
watching your tired, decisive calmness,
my bruised shin, which I've forgotten, starts to ache,
and I could hold this still moment forever:
the thick, antibody-rich sweetness of that first milk,
and the feeling of sensation returning,
drop by tentative drop.

The taste of river water

In a glowering afternoon
we duck through fences, stripping off sweaty clothes
to wade into the river's last deep spots.
Here, where the current
works painstakingly away at islands,
like a probing tongue encountering
a rough edge of a tooth.

The water laps my neck
my empty fingers break the purling surface.

It's intolerable
that everything I contain is calamitous,
that an insatiable hunger
still hooks its ruinous weights into me
bowing my shoulders like a harness,
intent on breaking me in;
it's an ache that waits
with all the time in the world —
your helpless eye, at last,
catches mine.

Both of us are braced here,
immersed inside this stirred-up chill;
in its submerged branches and dark shadowed holes
we can pretend ourselves baptised or buried
and that slow insistent pull, like fingers exploring torn muscle,
is the river bending around us, oblivious,
looking for a way through.

I have no answers, and nothing here could care less.
It is so delicate, and so calmly relentless,
this implacable current,
exposing the stiff swollen hinges of our longing.

My legs refuse to slip under,
to let me breathe water,
to be carried downstream, unresisting,
past these high ragged banks, eroded
by the flow of better years,
the high dry watermark of past seasons.

We gaze, emptied by silence,
then both cup a simultaneous hand into the water
and raise it to our mouths.

There is no blue plastic seal to crack
no faint, protective antibiotic assurance
this is river water.

In it, taste rain, eucalypt, sun,
the steeped bark of fallen boughs,
rust from dissolved barbed barriers,
tears
oxygen
earth

We recognise this taste
like the fence-line an outstretched hand finds in the dark;
yes, here: the soothing cool steel of the gate,

the ploughed soil ridged like fingerprints,
the brackish sediments settling.

These are our boundaries.
Our silenced mouths drink
humbled by lack of choice.

And here we stand, and here's the miracle of it:
we're somehow still thirsty,
braced dogged in the current
rooted in mud and leaves
still testing the hope
of weightlessness.

The test shows positive

We need a slow boat to rediscover our sea legs.
We cannot look back at the land we are leaving
distance making it deceptive
wreathed in softening green.

And how to chart a map detailed enough?
We would need a scale of one inch to an inch,
and unrolling it would cover the landscape.

Better to just take this crayon
and trace my outline,
gaze until when you close your eyes
it is there like a negative afterburn;
let those water edges
blur away with sweat and tears
let us both lose our bearings
so that we can scorn
such lame and stunted cartography.

I am hoarding moments with you
like limes against scurvy,
the comfort of your skin
and your low voice fielding phone calls downstairs,
forced to endure the telling of it over and over,
each remembered gentleness
lets my hands find the ropes
to secure these sails.

The surface stirs,
some breeze promised by the new moon is gathering

to swell the canvas,
the timbers knock, faint and rhythmic
as we sit shivering, waiting, for some white bird to wheel out
from a shore over the horizon,
so that this new imperative
can pull us as surely as a tide.

How grave your face is, when I break the news,
hiding, for fear of its terrible wonder,
its secret, unquenchable faith
in the New World.

Like a storm

Forty weeks swelling like a circus tent,
pulling on the rigging ropes
to bring it swaying and stretched to extravagant completion,
and now in lamplight
we marvel at the show

ringside seats for joy and terror
as beneath the rosy Big Top
you kick your heels under our trembling hands
every molecule perfect as you arch your back
acknowledge our upturned, awestruck faces
and swing
your daring trapeze somersaults

already a showstopper
under the taut canvas
already no-net
death-defying
ladies and gentlemen

the morning my waters broke
I was kneeling in the garden pulling up couch grass
and I felt you coming like a storm:
the promise of pleated grey cloud on the horizon
and in that small downpour that pattered onto the earth
I caught the beloved scent of you —
the sweet, sharp, forgotten tang
of the inland sea.

Thank you

Too tender to move from here
we lie in the bed, you and I
I study your fontanel
the soft hair swirling like a map of wind.

Below us
your father, again, makes call after call.

A girl
he says
a beautiful girl.
Yeah, all fine.
Thank you
he says
thank you

I have everything I need
I want nothing except a crystal vial
to save
every tear wept with joy.

The Zen master

I have written this
with a body stretched and sore,
stitches swollen, torn by a crowning head
tongue thick with painkillers
and in the next room a cry for milk
to set my heart off like a caged bird against my ribs.

And I have written this
dragging with me a lead apron of grainy exhaustion,
page prickling through a stinging mist
mouth metallic with adrenalin
while she sleeps, frowning, tender as a camellia.

I have written all I could,
in a gluttonous scrawling haste,
hearing her call for me, crawling through the other room
written it washed with guilt, the soup burned to the saucepan
snatching just five illicit minutes to myself,
for godsakes, just five.

And I have written
as she sat under my feet
pulling what's hoarded from the shelf below,
cringing at the sound of tearing paper
until the computer connection suddenly went dead
and she — gummy, triumphant, seated like the Buddha —
held the cable aloft, and waved it like a prayer flag.

And I have written, like today,
as she stood by my leg crying with frustration
beating a tattoo onto my thigh with both hands

her face transposing everything, urgently seeking my eyes
demanding I turn away from this pointless thing
because out there, the whole humming world is waiting.
See, says her fervent outstretched finger, *see there*
is the outside
trust me
everything you need is there.

Tell me you wouldn't rise,
given that call,
and follow her
helpless and ardent
as a chastened disciple.

Dawn service

Five a.m., and a hungry lamb wail from the cot
as the murmuring clock radio says it's Anzac Day.
The world belongs to war veterans and breastfeeding mothers,
all rising for the dawn service.

All of us in shared testimony to the same belief,
our minute's silence to what stays unacknowledged,
all the unfathomable, exhausted sacrifice
of our mutely bowed heads.

The baby's eyes, absorbed and concentrating,
stare over my shoulder as if there's something
of huge, ungraspable portent on the horizon —
men coming over battlements, say,
a rising sun cold as steel,
a glint of bayonets above the cliffs.

A tiny frown creases her forehead
and her hand jerks up and comes to rest
against her face.
We sit there milk-drunk, humming, somnolent,
the breaking dawn scudding like a prow towards the shore
and onwards, boys, to glory —

because there she lies, the quiet hard-won miracle of her
gazing past me at something beyond my vision
my perfect little opus.

There is no trumpet playing the last post, no drums.
Just her curving cheek,
unsullied and fragile and full of promise,

her slight but determined breathing
as she pulls all nourishment into herself,
and that small hand raising itself softly, insistently,
like an envoy stepping out into no-man's land
calling for peace.

Swimming class

At the other end of the hydro pool
the Special Needs Adults
float and call out through their aqua-aerobics session;
at this end is the Baby Swimming Class.

We mothers nurse our sturdy, solid-fleshed toddlers,
hold them close to us, buoyant, safe;
and smile back
at the unfocused smiles of the adults —
or at the closed-off gaze, looking past us —
and lower our perfect children
like a blessed baptism
into warm water.

This,
this paddling and kicking,
this taking of breaths,
this turning in the water and touching the side,
immerses all of us.

My hands are solicitous, conscientious,
beneath my child's tender armpits,
although I long to swim myself —
break free and kick to the far side,
slicing through water, remembering how to stretch,
my solitary rhythmic breathing slow and silver —
I tread water instead, and hold her
robust and sure as a dolphin.

Now she wants goggles,
now she wants to float, her head on my shoulder

and observe her own reflection, twisting like a mermaid
in the misted overhead mirror.

The disconnected shouts of the other group —
half-formed words, lost calls, whale songs —
bounce off the high, hangar ceiling.
They bat away our floating toys
and watch, incurious at first,
as we form ourselves and our babies into a circle
to sing *Old MacDonald.*

One girl paddles over
and waits humbly outside the circle,
and her carer guides her back;
no, Susan, over here, back here, Susan

but at the chorus, hesitant, remembering,
one by one they join in:
E-I-E-I-O!

The babies laugh as we thresh them through the water,
lift them streaming and squealing above our heads,
and we're all singing now
our voices, across the pool,
afloat and warm and out of tune,
miraculously weightless.

Our children's hands reach for us
like a benediction,
showing us the way
into the deep water.

III

Requeening

I stand in a column
Of winged, unmiraculous women,
Honey-drudgers ...
Sylvia Plath, 'Stings'

Oh, Sylvia, with your bee poems
and your fear of the boxed-up swarm
what would you have made of these hives,
sturdy and prosaic as filing cabinets
set among the river redgums?
The bees, clinging to the combs as the river rose,
all drowned last spring,
and today our resident apiarist is recolonising
humming in the sunshine
requeening.

You wouldn't recognise the process now.
The queens are mailed to you in the post
from the 'mating nucleus colony'
arriving in a small white box
with an entourage of escort workers.
At one end of the box is a small plug of queen candy
made of irradiated honey and icing sugar.
You will love this: in the days it takes
for the bees to eat their way through the candy
to release the queen
they learn to love her.
They stroke and feed her through the gauze mesh
stimulating her to produce the pheromones she needs
for them to worship her rather than kill her.

Would you stand here as I do, Sylvia, dizzy with metaphor
watching the bees swooping in on the breeze
eating their way in to her,
the empty comb waiting like a thousand bridal beds
to be repopulated until she is exhausted?

Would you wonder if she is actually eating her way out
as you had to do,
trapped behind a solid wall of white sugar,
force-fed that surfeit of sweetness
the drudgery of crawling through
always ahead of you
as your body's warring chemicals, seething and trembling,
waited to find out
whether you were to be crowned or destroyed?

Temporality

I'll ask you to assemble here
next to the step where so many feet have stood shifting,
waiting for a welcome,
that they have worn a cupped impression in the brick.

There are no headphones or podcast,
no virtual tour
nothing is animatronic
there are not even signs;
in this museum objects must be noticed
in order to be named.

Let me invite you
to put your sceptical fingers here, into a wall
cracked open like a seam;
in that arid subsiding spot,
with its bite of jagged mortar exposed,
feel the evidence, deliberate as a glacier,
of movement
of the power of slow ruin.

And in the shed on this salvaged beam
taken from the old factory, you can read
the faded names of workers from half a century ago
still scrawled, provisionally, in pencil:
Joe Wally Gavin Terry

This four-inch nail banged in beside them to hold invoices
that they always meant to replace with a decent hook or clip;
see how it's still holding fast
long after they have gone,

see how they were wrong
about what was temporary.

These are the exhibits worth naming,
the triumph of the nondescript
the steady rise and rise
of the inevitable.

Seeing them here, barely visible, demanding nothing,
might remind you of your own belongings —
the last things you expected to have bundled under your arm;
the shirts washed colourless, and the unfinished books
that you know would have done you good,
one hand clutching the dented pie dish, scored
like an endless unsolved equation,
the hat with its forgotten tidemarks of sweat,
everything it's too late to grieve for
that you thought you had discarded,
everything you used, unthinkingly,
until it was burnished
into invisibility,
these remnants, adrift from their stories,
will end up here too.

Whatever lies we tell ourselves,
these are the things that will outlive us:
that brick
will see us out;
that forgotten nail
driven in with four heedless, glinting hammer blows
back in 1957

will remain immoveable in that piece of hardwood
when you and I are dust.

And the ghosts who've stopped in this doorway
and rested one hand tiredly against the wall
to take off their boots before coming inside —
just here, their fingers grazing this worn unsanctified spot —
their voices are as distant
as impossible
as sirens.

Well, this is where I leave you
to make your way through the rooms,
threading back and back into the hushed corners,
your lips moving with recognition,
until there are no rooms
until you are standing empty-handed
in the sunlight.

The blessing of the ring

The jeweller who took the ring I had been given
scrutinised the chipped stone
and said, *Well, it's a dress ring, that's the trouble.*

For a second I had a vision of a velvet box on a glass table,
and me, selecting a ring before an evening engagement
with cool and elegant hands.

Then he handed it back, and I recalled
the countless times I'd flown swearing down the stairs
to get the phone,
the back of my hand slamming into the wall on the way,
the pale blue opal cracking
along some fault line I'd doubtless caused
washing up in hot water, say, or slamming a bolt
carelessly home.

Finally, one day, holding a spade,
I glanced down at my left hand
to see the stone gone entirely;
dropped somewhere in this garden's upturned dirt
loosed from its moorings
the setting just four foolish empty claws, gripping nothing.

I think of it adrift now,
a tiny, flawed planet in orbit
turning its curved opalescent side to the light.

It could have happened anywhere, but by accident
I planted it here.

Now on nights I can't sleep I step outside
to check on that inky silhouette of cleared earth
and imagine the stone, like me
something small and hard and chipped,
making its slow haphazard way through this dark galaxy,
flung clear and tumbling, refracting light
as someone far above
is digging, always digging.

Makeover

The one certainty is that whatever you want to reveal
will be covered in lead-based paint.
When you apply the heat gun
it smells like the fumes could kill you.

Sometimes you find your eyes fill with tears,
your head spinning with nauseating stars;
after a while your hand aches
just with scraping.

Re-entering the room,
you stop in your tracks
think: *is this it?*

Occasionally your hand (the muscles remembering)
will sweep over it gently
and there will be a residue, flakes of paint.
You'll have to live with it now.

So step back and get it in perspective
get a hammer and nail and hang a picture there
or just keep banging until
you knock your way into another room.

Is there natural light?
Could you make a home here?
That's the question you will ask yourself,
standing ghostly with plaster dust
absently swinging your hammer, a great new idea
suddenly occurring to you.

October 14th, 2010: the Chilean miners are lifted into the light

First out is Florencio Avalos, a man alive after sixty-nine days,
who hugs his sobbing son and thanks his president.
Trapped men wait patiently below
under two thousand feet of rock at Esperanza.

Then comes the exultant cry of Mario Sepulveda —
the clown of the imprisoned group,
the singer, the stalwart —
the cold sun blazes as he is pulled through the cavity
no wider than his own shoulders.

He removes the dark glasses they have given him,
so that his newborn eyes might filter the brutal glare,
and pulls off his oxygen mask
to let his lungs breathe air.

How to begin this story?
The president is waiting;
Mario Sepulveda turns and sees him
through a nebula of shimmering, dilatory light.
'I have brought gifts,' he says and begins to hand out
the offerings he has prepared and held clutched to his chest
through the cooling darkness to the surface —
pieces of rock he has collected from the tunnel in the earth,
rocks for the seventeen days without a sound
when his family presumed him dead,
the fifty-two days afterwards.

Mario Sepulveda has wrapped the rocks in silver foil.
One by one he presents to each official, each journalist,

then the president himself
a small piece of the earth he has prised free.
The president embraces him, the better to hide his tears;
the national flag snaps in the wind.
'I have been with God and the devil,' says Sepulveda,
'and I seized the hand of God. It was the better hand.'

Below him, thirty-one men still wait their turn
for the lowering of the Phoenix capsule,
and the ascent back through the shaft,
and each man emerging, one by one,
into the bright and haloed air.

We are well in the refuge the thirty-three,
their first note had read.
Now the stones,
gouged from far beneath them and carried to the surface,
are held in the world's uncertain hands
as though, at any moment, they might speak.

Manuel Gonzalez, the first rescuer to have reached the men,
remains alone underground while the capsule
bears aloft the last miner, Luis Urzua,
who for those first seventeen days of no word and no sign
fed each of the men a spoonful of tuna and a sip of milk
and, even now, waited till last.

Gonzalez can hear through his earpiece
the applause from the surface two kilometres above,
and knows they are each safely delivered.

Before he climbs inside for his own slow journey
through the smooth-walled silent tunnel
a camera records him pausing:

he turns back to the hacked womb of rock
and bows.

Letter (2)

This gesture
of slapping each pocket
searching for a stray piece of paper
as the moment flies past, perfect, like a shooting star

is like trying to put yourself out
when you suddenly realise you're on fire

because there you'll be
watching your daughter dancing in a square of sunlight

and what you'll remember —
and here's the confounding part —
is leaning out over a high parapet
an updraft lifting your hair

(dancing in a square of sunlight
and every clap sending up crested pigeons
like a magician, card after card
appearing)

yes, the high ledge of the Sagrada Familia cathedral,
having taken the stairs spiralling like the bones in an ear
and even here Antoni Gaudi
has covered the stone with mosaic tiles

and if you lean out further, to the thrilling tipping point
(ledge grating against your pelvic bones,
but it's OK, because you're immortal,
thin, twenty-three and travelling Europe)
if you lean on that upswelling air and crane your neck

to look under the curve of this corkscrewing spire
you will see he has written you a secret message, in mosaic,
that says *gloria, gloria, gloria*

heavy-footed now, struck dumb, you watch her
while she pirouettes,
and in every crack of her small ecstatic hands
you hear Gaudi
breaking tiles and teacups
the exultant humming
of reassembly —

which is why I am writing this now,
from fragments scrawled on an envelope
that say *wings*
and *sagrada familia*
and *remember leaning out*

better to just bring it to you,
out of breath and hurrying
to press this envelope into your hands
before the braided filament of it fades

listen:
every clap is like a wingbeat
and God's architect
once climbed out into thin air over the city
to shout his praises to glory.